Best Behavior™

Excuse me, but it's my turn.....

Written by Karen Romano Young
Illustrated by Doug Cushman

ideals®
Nelson Place at Elm Hill Pike
Nashville, Tennessee 37214

Titles in the Best Behavior™ Series

Published by Ideals Publishing Corporation

Produced for Ideals Publishing Corporation by
Joshua Morris Publishing, Inc.
167 Old Post Road, Southport, Connecticut 06490

Printed in Singapore

Someone famous once said, "It's not whether you win or lose, it's how you play the game." Manners have a lot to do with how you play the game.

Before you make the team. . .

Sports require good manners, before, during, and after the game. This is especially true when you play on a team. First, you may have to try out for a team. Just try to do your best.

Don't make excuses for your mistakes.

Player's from last year's team may have to try out again. If someone tries to upset you, don't pay attention.

I'm ALWAYS the goalie, kid!

Likewise, if you're a member of last year's team, don't show off.

What if you don't make the team? Quietly decide to practice extra hard next time. Give yourself time to get over your disappointment before deciding you'll never play again.

Don't go around complaining about the way the tryouts were run.

Once you've made the team. . .
Take responsibility for being a good team member.

Don't miss practice if you can help it. If you have to miss practice, be sure and call your coach. Don't expect your parents to do it for you (unless you're too sick to come to the phone). Be a team player.

Be a team player. Be willing to learn, listen, and try new things at your coach's suggestion.

On the way to the game. . .

Don't distract the bus driver by running around the bus or by singing too loud.

Don't scream out the windows or throw things at passing cars and people.

If you travel in a carpool, be respectful toward the driver. If you need a ride home from the school, field, or pick-up place, ask someone ahead of time if possible.

At the game. . .

Keep quiet about the other team's field, court, town, locker room, etc.

Never make rude comments.

Say 'good luck' to the other team.

Cheer for your team.

If you kick or hit the ball over a fence or into the woods, volunteer to get it yourself.

If you're stuck on the bench, don't sulk. Instead, watch the game and cheer your team on. Be ready to join the game as soon as your coach needs you.

Don't be a star. No one makes a touchdown, goal, or basket without the team behind them. Never brag about yourself!

Fans can be difficult. If your parents (or other friends and relatives) make you embarrassed, politely ask them to be more quiet.

Ask your coach to handle problems with other team members, parents, or friends.

If someone is injured, get them the help they need as soon as possible, or help them off the field.

Don't crowd around a hurt person.

Don't discuss the person's injury with others if you really don't know what happened. You could frighten someone or start a rumor.

Many people think it's smart or cool to argue with the referee or umpire. In almost all cases, the ref will not change their mind. Besides, arguing is against the rules of most games. You could be thrown out or forced to give up the game to the other team.

Never cheat.

If you suspect someone of cheating, quietly mention it to your coach. Let the coach speak to the referee or handle the problem himself.

Never. . .

. . .use bad language,

. . .fight with the other players,

. . .insult other players,

. . .tackle or bump someone in order to hurt them.

These things are impolite, and they show that you are a poor sport. What's more, they're against the rules.

After the game. . .

Shake hands with the other players and coaches, or give them a team cheer.

Be a gracious winner,

Even if you're the most valuable player, the win belongs to the whole team.

Be a brave loser. Don't complain about the rules, the coach, the other players, or the field. Instead congratulate the winners.

If possible, smile.

Be considerate of the person who cleans your uniform. Hand it over as soon as possible after the game.

Other sports. . .

Some sports have fewer rules. Still, manners are important.

Play where you won't disturb anyone. Whether you play on a school playground or in a public park don't hog the whole area.

Don't hog equipment meant to be shared by all.

Let others join you if they want.

Generally, the people who start the game set the rules. If you join in the game later, don't argue about the rules.

When Hiking. . .

. . .follow marked trails,
. . .stay with your group, don't wander off by yourself,
. . .don't litter or destroy any plants or trees.

. . .be considerate of other hikers. Don't make too much noise or frighten other people.

When Skiing. . .

. . .stay on marked trails,
. . .ski at a safe speed,
. . .don't cut into the lift line.

If you save a place for a friend, ask the people behind you if they mind if your friend joins you.

When swimming. . .

. . .pay attention to the lifeguard,
. . .don't run around the deck of the pool,
. . .don't push people into the pool for fun,
. . .watch out for the other swimmers, expecially younger
    children.

When jogging. . .

Stay to the side of a busy sidewalk or road. Better yet, find a
place that isn't crowded.

If you're behind a group that is blocking your path, slow down
and call out "Excuse me." If they don't move, stop and walk
around them.

Using manners as part of sports doesn't mean you can't have fun. It means that everyone can enjoy themselves in their own way!